THE TWENTIETH– CENTURY WAY

Tom Jacobson

BROADWAY PLAY PUBLISHING INC
224 E 62nd St, NY, NY 10065
www.broadwayplaypub.com
info@broadwayplaypub.com

THE TWENTIETH–CENTURY WAY
© Copyright 2012 by Tom Jacobson

First printing: November 2012
I S B N: 978-0-88145-535-9

Book design: Marie Donovan
Word processing: Microsoft Word
Typographic controls: Xerox Ventura Publisher 2.0 P E
Typeface: Palatino
Printed and bound in the U S A

THE TWENTIETH-CENTURY WAY was first
produced at The Theater @ Boston Court (Jessica
Kubzansky and Michael Michetti, Artistic Directors,
and Michael Seel, Executive Director) running from
29 April to 20 June, 2010. The cast and creative
contributors were:

BROWN... Will Bradley
WARREN ....Robert Mammana

Director...Michael Michetti
Scenic & properties design.............................Nick Santiago
Lighting design .... Elizabeth Harper
Costume design...Garry Lennon
Sound design.. Kari Rae Seekins
Dialect coach ....Tracy Winters
Assistant director...Sabina Ptasznik
Production stage manager .... Amber Koehler
Casting director .... Michael Donovan, CSA
Key art..Christopher Komuro

CHARACTERS

BROWN
WARREN

The following must be included in the program of all productions of THE TWENTIETH-CENTURY WAY:

Author's Note: I am deeply grateful to Lillian Faderman and Stuart Timmons for their book *Gay L A*, my first encounter with Warren and Brown. I am indebted to scholar Sharon Ullman who brought this story to light originally in her 1995 article "The Twentieth Century Way: Female Impersonation and Sexual Practice in Turn of the Century America" (Journal of the History of Sexuality, Volume 5 Number 4, [April 1995] 573-600) and delved into it further in Chapter 3, "The Twentieth Century Way" of her book *Sex Seen: The Emergence of Modern Sexuality in America* (University of California Press 1997). I studied her findings with great interest as I undertook the writing of the play. Those who uncover and interpret important historical events that highlight the often forcibly buried complexity of the past provide the building blocks to so much artistic work.

(BROWN *sits, waiting. He is dressed in slightly flashy lower middle class clothes circa 1914. After a moment,* WARREN *comes in, dressed identically. They study each other from a distance.* WARREN *walks up to* BROWN, *too close, a challenge.* BROWN *does not move, refusing to be intimidated.* WARREN *picks lint off of* BROWN's *suit.)*

WARREN: *(New York accent)* Sharp.

BROWN: *(Shrugs, Chicago accent)* They said dress up.

WARREN: City slicker.

BROWN: I'm from—

WARREN: The job. City Slicker?

BROWN: I guess.

WARREN: You haven't prepared?

BROWN: I was only told—is this the right place? I've been waiting—

WARREN: How long?

BROWN: You're the only other—are you? —is this normal?

WARREN: You took the time to dress up but didn't bother to research?

BROWN: He's a confidence man.

WARREN: You might as well go home now.

BROWN: You prepared? Researched—?

WARREN: He's a very particular confidence man,
a product of his time, his environment, a victim of
circumstance, like the Progressives say.

BROWN: The Progressives? C'mon!

WARREN: For instance, this confidence man would
know what happened June 28, 1914.

BROWN: The assassination of Archduke Ferdinand.
Everybody knows that.

WARREN: You'd be surprised by common ignorance.
June 6, 1914.

BROWN: First airplane flight from Los Angeles to San
Francisco.

WARREN: You keep up.

BROWN: I live in Los Angeles.

WARREN: Who is widely regarded as the last castrato?

BROWN: How can you imagine I'd know that?

WARREN: So you don't?

BROWN: Alessandro Moreschi. You should hear the *Ave
Maria* he recorded in 1905. Unearthly. How many were
killed in the Chinese Massacre of 1871?

WARREN: Eighteen—

BROWN: Ah! Nineteen—!

WARREN: —Eighteen men—

BROWN & WARREN: —And one boy.

WARREN: Your grasp of history is nearly as impressive
as mine.

BROWN: Perhaps we are the same person.

WARREN: That smacks of vanity, sir.

BROWN: In my character or yours? You're not *that*
good-looking.

WARREN: One's looks are less compelling than knowledge, craft and keen observation. I perceive such a glimmer in you, my friend. You are avid for... connection. What do you know about Marie Dressler?

BROWN: Born November 9, 1868 in Ontario, Canada, Marie Dressler made her debut on Broadway in 1892 and by 1900 was a vaudeville star. She started her motion picture career with Mack Sennett—

WARREN: *(Halting him with a gesture)* Tell me about *Tillie's Punctured Romance.*

BROWN: It's supposed to be a comedy, but it's not a very funny script.

WARREN: Why not?

BROWN: A cad deceiving a woman. That's more mean than funny.

WARREN: We're not really meant to empathize with Tillie, just laugh at her from a distance. Comedy engages the mind, tragedy the emotions.

BROWN: So cruelty is funny?

(WARREN knocks him down. BROWN is stunned.)

BROWN: That's not funny! Shit!

WARREN: But they're laughing— *(Refers to audience)* —Out there. At least in their hearts.

(BROWN picks himself up, now more wary of WARREN.)

BROWN: Your approach is decidedly low-brow.

WARREN: On the contrary, I've studied the Delsarte System of Expression.

BROWN: What's that?

WARREN: *(Demonstrates)* Certain physical movements are tied to emotions—

BROWN: How nineteenth century! All that ridiculous— *(Poses melodramatically)* —Posing!

WARREN: Outer expressiveness leads to true characterization.

BROWN: I'd rather work outward from inner truth—

WARREN: Ah, Stanislavsky—

BROWN: —Than flail about— *(Flails)* —With Monsieur Delsarte.

WARREN: We have a fundamental difference of opinion.

BROWN: Indeed.

WARREN: In which motion pictures have you appeared?

BROWN: I most recently played Othello—

WARREN: Othello? Really? On stage?

(BROWN nods.)

WARREN: Where—?

(BROWN starts to say.)

WARREN: No—I can guess. *(With an exaggerated Chicago accent)* Chicago.

BROWN: Thank you, Henry Higgins.

WARREN: You should work on that. Develop a neutral accent so people don't type you.

BROWN: What about you, with that Bronx—?

WARREN: It's Brooklyn— *(Drops the accent)* And I can drop it whenever I want. It's all about vocal variation. I'm not one of those actors who can only play themselves.

BROWN: *(English accent)* Now by heaven,
My blood begins my safer guides to rule,

And passion, having my best judgments collied,
Assays to lead the way. Tis monstrous, Iago.

WARREN: *(English)* Hah! I like not that.

BROWN: What dost thou say?

WARREN: Nothing, my lord; or if—I know not what.

BROWN: Is he not honest?

WARREN: Honest, my lord?

BROWN: Honest? Ay, honest.

WARREN: My lord, for aught I know.

BROWN: What dost thou think?

WARREN: Think, my lord?

BROWN: Think, my lord? By heaven, thou echo'st me,
As if there were some monster in thy thought
Too hideous to be shown!

WARREN: Who in the world cast you as Othello?

BROWN: Impressive Iago. But you skipped almost an
entire page. *(He looks smug.)*

WARREN: Might I recognize your name?

BROWN: It's—

WARREN: Don't tell me. Whatever it is, I hope it's more
neutral than your voice.

BROWN: It's—

WARREN: No! You need a nice, general-sounding
American name that qualifies you to play any role.
Nothing too foreign that could type you by country
like Costello, Bergman, Kaczmarek—

BROWN: It's—

WARREN: Brown.

BROWN: Brown?

WARREN: Resolutely uninflected, bland, even as a color. Beige is more neutral, and taupe practically disappears, but both sound too French. Brown it is.

BROWN: You peeked at the sign-in. And who are you, sir?

WARREN: Not important.

BROWN: Know thy...competition.

WARREN: My name is Warren.

(Offers his hand.)

BROWN: *(Shaking)* Brown.

WARREN: You're not going to get the role, you know.

BROWN: Why not?

WARREN: Neither am I.

BROWN: I'm sure we're both qualified.

WARREN: I'm too ruggedly handsome.

(BROWN *reacts.*)

WARREN: And you're too— *(Looks him up and down)* Pretty.

BROWN: Pretty?!

WARREN: Surely you've heard that before. No one hesitates to tell actors what's wrong with them.

BROWN: Pretty—all the time.

WARREN: Use it! Use what you've got. There are lots of roles for pretty actors. Just not this one.

BROWN: He could be a pretty city slicker.

WARREN: Confidence men are neither pretty nor ruggedly handsome. They are charming but disappear with the loot. They are taupe, beige—

BROWN: Brown.

WARREN: Too pretty, just the same. It's all about the look.

BROWN: Surface.

(WARREN *nods. Neither moves.*)

BROWN: They said to wait here.

WARREN: How long ago?

BROWN: Not too long.

WARREN: Minutes?

BROWN: Um—

WARREN: Hours?

BROWN: Two. And a half. Is that typical?

WARREN: This is your first movie audition, isn't it?

BROWN: Yes. Yours?

WARREN: You wanna get a drink?

BROWN: Um—

WARREN: I've got a new bottle of Chartreuse at my apartment.

BROWN: What's that?

WARREN: I'm astonished, Mister Brown, student of history—

BROWN: I'm not a student of history—if I hear something once, I have it memorized. I can't help it.

WARREN: Then I'm even more astonished that you're unfamiliar with the famed liqueur developed by the Carthusian monks—

BROWN: Liqueur? Sounds effeminate, if you don't mind my saying. Is it sweet?

WARREN: It's manly sweet. Not everyone can handle it.

BROWN: I'd rather not, thanks. I'm not ready to give up here.

WARREN: Then I shall stay as well.

BROWN: You were trying to trick me into leaving!

WARREN: Ever study *commedia del arte*?

BROWN: What's that?

WARREN: You know the history of everything but your own craft. It's Italian improvisation from the 16th century.

BROWN: I don't want to get an accent.

WARREN: You memorize without effort, even Shakespeare, and you versify smoothly. But improvisation requires different skills.

BROWN: Such as what?

WARREN: Let's just do it and you'll see. Winner stays—

(At the same time:)

WARREN: —Loser goes—

BROWN: Winner—?

WARREN: The better actor wins the right to stay and audition.

BROWN: *(Smiling)* That's a bet I can make.

WARREN: Bed?

BROWN: Bet!

(WARREN offers BROWN his hand. BROWN shakes.)

WARREN: First, we must set some limits. Our time is 1914.

BROWN: *(Not quite understanding)* Very well...

WARREN: The early years of the twentieth century. That way we can keep wearing what we've got. Social change is sweeping the nation—

BROWN: The world!

WARREN: Exactly. But let me set the scene, if you please. We also need a problem.

BROWN: A problem?

WARREN: The heart of improvisation is solving a problem. Sometimes it's simply that your fellow thespian has dropped a line and you must improvise dialogue to get the scene back on track. But our problem is: vice!

BROWN: Vice?

WARREN: At the dawn of the twentieth century, vice swept the nation—

BROWN: The world!

WARREN: Health and cleanliness increased, thanks to Progressive reforms—

BROWN: This led to vice?

WARREN: Tell me about your grandfather's dick.

BROWN: Beg pardon?

WARREN: Your grandfather's dick. Did you ever see it?

BROWN: No! Why would I see that?

WARREN: You'll get nowhere as an actor with the imagination of a school marm. Improvise!

BROWN: Wrinkly. And pale. But really, really big! It runs in the family.

WARREN: Did you ever see him clean it?

BROWN: *(Horrified)* No!

WARREN: As public hygiene improved in the twentieth century, smegma went into retreat. The aforementioned Progressives fought for public bathing facilities to tidy the unwashed masses streaming through Ellis Island. Widespread residential plumbing followed.

BROWN: People got cleaner. What's that to do with vice?

WARREN: Everything, Mister Brown! Cleaner bodies meant cleaner dicks. Clean enough to eat off of.

BROWN: You possess irrepressible style, Mister Warren.

WARREN: While fellatio was only christened with a formal Latin name in 1893, the practice was well-known throughout recorded history. But with the demise of the cheesy dick, new life was breathed into old vice.

BROWN: What are you after, sir?

WARREN: In crowded cities full of men rushing between sweatshop and home, a quick oral satisfaction is distinctly more convenient than anal penetration.

BROWN: Anal penetration! I suspect you are no longer speaking of men and women.

WARREN: I never was. The vice of fellatio is sodomy as a snack.

BROWN: Repulsive.

WARREN: Vile. Hazardous as well.

BROWN: How so?

WARREN: (*Audibly clicks his teeth in a scary way*) Danger is part of the attraction.

BROWN: And this problem will be solved by improvisation?

WARREN: We are in California, are we not?

BROWN: Indeed.

WARREN: Where, in 1914, fellatio is not a felony, while sodomy is.

BROWN: But it's prosecuted, is it not?

WARREN: Rarely, and only as "social vagrancy."

BROWN: What's that to do with us and our improvisation?

WARREN: You are not wealthy, I presume.

BROWN: *(Shrugs)* I'm an actor.

WARREN: You'd do anything for money.

BROWN: Well, now, not absolutely—

WARREN: Fearlessness is the actor's sharpest tool, Mister Brown. If you are impecunious—

BROWN: I'm not afraid to reveal myself, especially to one similarly afflicted. I need this role. I am well nigh desperate.

WARREN: My sympathies. And yet one of us will not get the part.

BROWN: So what have we to offer each other?

WARREN: In the long term, that remains to be seen. In the short term, I have a proposition for you.

BROWN: Beg pardon?

WARREN: A business proposition. Don't be disgusting.

BROWN: My mistake.

WARREN: Business is identifying a need and fulfilling it.

BROWN: You see a need in vice?

WARREN: In its eradication. As the Progressives rail against prostitution, the public revulsion for the new old vice of oral sodomy grows daily.

BROWN: How may an actor root out vice?

WARREN: With skills the common man does not possess.

BROWN: This is beginning to feel unwholesome.

WARREN: We're merely improvising. But for cash.

BROWN: An example, if you please.

WARREN: I wasn't always an actor. I was once an investigative reporter for *The New York Times.*

BROWN: Now you are most assuredly improvising. Show me a by-line, sir.

WARREN: Much of what I wrote was not fit to print. I knew every pestilent tavern in Manhattan, every noisome watering hole where vice grew like mold on cheese.

BROWN: You mix a vulgar metaphor, Mister Warren.

WARREN: One particular establishment, The Slide, was notorious, with queer shows and boys for sale in bulk like chickens. I learned their habits. And turned them to my advantage.

BROWN: In a lucrative manner, I presume?

WARREN: Then you have an interest, Mister Brown?

BROWN: Not in white slavery, if that's your meaning. But, like you, I am not, at the moment, a wealthy man.

WARREN: Is blackmail beneath your station?

BROWN: Are we—improvising—now?

WARREN: If I say we are, then we're not.

BROWN: Because it sounds mean.

WARREN: Mean? Stamping out sin? Liquidating lasciviousness? Why, Mister Brown, it's nothing less than a public service. A moral duty!

BROWN: Am I to understand that you—in some fashion—ape the vice in order to attract it?

WARREN: Then spring my trap—before defilement.

BROWN: Why, Mister Warren, that's deceit!

WARREN: *(Triumphant)* No—acting!

BROWN: If that's acting, I'm not at all certain the craft is a worthy enterprise. Clearly not a significant contribution to society, and not what I'd want to do with the rest of my life.

WARREN: It's terribly significant! Urgent! To act is to take action!

BROWN: And definitely not at all fun.

WARREN: I guarantee fun.

BROWN: I could never do anything like that. It's immoral in every possible way.

WARREN: But that's your advantage as an actor. You're not immoral—you're playing the role of the person who's immoral.

(BROWN *contemplates.*)

WARREN: Just follow my lead. (*He goes to the costume rack and selects some pieces.*)

BROWN: What?

WARREN: We're merely improvising, Mister Brown. You will not be compromised.

(WARREN *puts a police cap on* BROWN's *head.*)

BROWN: I can't—I'm not ready—

WARREN: Don't tempt me to doubt your skills, sir. I win by default.

BROWN: But—who—?

WARREN: If you knew everything in advance, it wouldn't be improvisation, would it?

BROWN: But the rules—?

WARREN: Just play along!

BROWN: But I—

WARREN: Chief Cole, my name is Warren, and I have a business proposition for you.

BROWN: Pardon?

WARREN: *(Sotto voce)* Find him in a gesture.
(Demonstrates)

BROWN: What? No!

WARREN: A community policing model tested on the rough and tumble streets of New York City.

BROWN: *(Struggling to find his character without gesture)* You don't say?

WARREN: Why would this be of interest, you might ask.

BROWN: *(After a moment, in a COLE voice)* Why would this be of interest? To me, sir?

WARREN: To the Long Beach Police Department? Well, let me tell you.

BROWN/COLE: *(Fully invested in the character)* Proceed, Mister Warren.

WARREN: As a former vice reporter for *The New York Times*, I've observed our urban areas blighted by crimes repellent in the extreme.

BROWN/COLE: Crimes against nature?

WARREN: Precisely, sir! Then the problem is as prevalent in this fair western city as in the metropolis of the east?

BROWN/COLE: It is a concern, sir, much to my discredit.

WARREN: I have a solution, Chief Cole, that will rid Long Beach of public vice in one year or less.

BROWN/COLE: I am on tenterhooks.

WARREN: My partner, Mister Brown, and I—

BROWN/COLE: Where is your partner, Mister Warren?

WARREN: Researching, sir, the dens of vice in your city, the low taverns, the shady parks, the bathing houses, the public pissoirs—

BROWN/COLE: Yes, the problem is pervasive. What is your solution, Mister Warren?

WARREN: I'm delighted you agree. My partner and I have studied this population, men given to this sort of thing, and we not only know where they gather, like vultures around carrion, but also how to apprehend them.

BROWN/COLE: We try, but they flee, sir. These gentlemen are a wary lot.

WARREN: They are skilled at escape, Houdinis of abomination, and have learnt a new method of conducting their debauches.

BROWN/COLE: What might that be, sir?

WARREN: First, a demonstration—

(Reaches for his crotch.)

BROWN/COLE: Mister Warren, that's quite unnecessary.

WARREN: I'll wager it's something you've not seen before.

BROWN/COLE: That does not mean I'm anxious to see it.

WARREN: Be not faint-hearted, sir!

BROWN/COLE: I'm not faint-hearted, I'm a police chief.

WARREN: Then—behold!

(WARREN unzips his zipper. BROWN/COLE just stares. WARREN zips it back up, pauses, then zips it down again with great flair.)

BROWN/COLE: What are you showing me, Mister Warren?

WARREN: It's a "separable fastener," invented just last year by a man named Gideon Sundback. *(Zips up, then down.)*

Zip, zip, zip! A gentle purring sound. And much faster than trouser buttons.

BROWN/COLE: It is indeed a convenience.

WARREN: I can see in your eye you recognize the implications.

BROWN/COLE: The device offers quick—

WARREN: Access—to the genital region. Exactly, sir, you have grasped it! Practitioners of vice are already rushing to purchase this technological wonder to abet their wickedness. If they are caught *in flagrante,* they simply— *(Zips up)* Zip up—and off they run. A tidal wave of perversion is poised to crash upon your shores.

BROWN/COLE: Have you dramatic training, Mister Warren?

WARREN: Not at all, Chief Cole. My training has been solely of the moral variety. Do you suspect me of exaggeration?

BROWN/COLE: You've escalated your crotch to a national crisis.

WARREN: They're already calling it "The Twentieth–Century Way."

BROWN/COLE: Calling what?

WARREN: Oral vice. *(Zips a few times)*

BROWN/COLE: That is sufficient, Mister Warren. I'm developing vertigo.

WARREN: But I have the solution! This little marking pen—indelible ink— *(Pulls out a marking pen.)*

BROWN/COLE: What's that for? No, don't tell me. Please go. You've wasted enough of my day.

WARREN: I propose a pilot program.

(BROWN/COLE *just stares.)*

WARREN: You needn't pay us a penny until my partner and I have brought ten of these reprobates to justice. And then—only fifteen dollars a head.

BROWN/COLE: If this got out—

WARREN: Absolutely clandestine, you have my word.

BROWN/COLE: I can't do this officially—

WARREN: Certainly not. But once you've cleaned the streets, imagine the approbation. Especially if Long Beach is the first city in the nation—

BROWN/COLE: Very well, Mister Warren. On a trial basis only.

(WARREN *is stupefied for a moment with joy, then rips the police cap off* BROWN *and drags him into a celebratory dance.*)

WARREN: Fifteen dollars a head! Fifteen dollars!

BROWN: That's a fortune!

WARREN: The easiest money you'll ever make!

BROWN: *(Pulling away from* WARREN*)* I haven't said I'll do it.

WARREN: Look, he even gave us these—

(Shows two badges. BROWN *takes one.)*

WARREN: I had them engraved.

BROWN: *(Reading)* "Special Vice Officer." *(Pins it on himself)* How very official.

WARREN: Inside, Mister Brown— *(Pins the badge to the inside of* BROWN'*s jacket)* Inside. You flash it only after you've obtained the evidence and captured the criminal. *(Demonstrates)* Special Vice Officer—

BROWN: *(Flashing similarly)* You're under arrest.

(BROWN *and* WARREN *laugh.*)

BROWN: *(Wary)* But it's only a role.

WARREN: Like any other. Othello, Iago, Special Vice Officer Brown. Now we must pursue our quarry.

BROWN: Where? Public pissoirs?

WARREN: Eventually. But first you must be trained.

BROWN: To do what?

WARREN: To seduce.

BROWN: Oh, no—

WARREN: Acting! *(He goes to the costume rack.)*

BROWN: Even so, Mister Warren—

(WARREN comes back with a dandyish costume piece or accessory.)

WARREN: Let your costume inspire!

(WARREN adds the costume piece to a reluctant BROWN.)

BROWN: You're turning me into one of those queer fellows!

WARREN: Yes, but we mustn't go too far. Ambiguity must be maintained. It attracts 'em. Most importantly, you can't tip 'em off you're a cop.

BROWN: *(Realizing)* I'm a cop!

WARREN: So you drop hints. Hairpins, they call 'em.

BROWN: Such as what?

WARREN: Something only that kind would know.

BROWN: Well, I don't know that, then.

WARREN: Ask me about Frederick Purssord.

BROWN: Who's that?

WARREN: Someone only that kind would know.

BROWN: How should I ask it?

WARREN: As one of them. Insinuatingly.

BROWN: *(Without flair)* You ever heard of Frederick Purssord?

WARREN: Oh, no, Mister Brown, where is your lilt, your flair, your cadence? You know how they speak! *(Demonstrates)* And gesture!

BROWN: I don't. I never met a one.

WARREN: *(Astonished)* And you're an actor?

BROWN: Not for certain, anyways.

WARREN: For any role—this or the Chief of Police—you must find in yourself a mannerism, a posture, an accent to externalize the character.

BROWN: Not that character I can't.

WARREN: Your Mister Stanislavsky would call it empathy.

BROWN: Even if you disapprove of the character and his actions? How can you feel for someone—

WARREN: You don't have to feel, just act like you do. That's the trick, and making the audience feel the same—

BROWN: Twisting their expectations?

WARREN: Once again, follow my lead. Ask me again about Purssord in that unconvincing way of yours.

BROWN: *(A bit better)* So...by the way...do you happen to know Frederick Purssord?

WARREN: *(Suddenly campy)* Know? You mean *knew*!

BROWN: *(Adopting a bit of WARREN's tone)* Knew, of course.

WARREN: So sad.

BROWN: Terrible, terrible.

WARREN: One day practicing his nude electric therapy, the next—

BROWN: Oh, I know!

WARREN: —Hung himself in jail!

BROWN: Poor fellow.

WARREN: Did you ever visit that hotel he owned?

BROWN: Which is that?

WARREN: The Merced. All male residents.

BROWN: Oh, yes, I believe I did. A lively establishment.

WARREN: They do all the latest dances. So romantic!

BROWN: If you want to stay *au courant*—

BROWN & WARREN: Visit the Merced!

WARREN: That's where I learned the foxtrot.

BROWN: What's that?

WARREN: Oh, just the latest! A dance invented by Mister Harry Fox in New York City at the New Amsterdam Roof Garden on the night of July 28, 1914.

BROWN: You don't say!

WARREN: *(Sotto voce, coaching)* Ask me how it goes.

BROWN: How does that one go?

WARREN: *(Manipulating BROWN)* The lady puts her right hand here, and her left here. Then the gentleman holds her firmly, thus—

BROWN: *(Trying to pull away)* Ah—Mister—

WARREN: *(Leading)* Then, with the lady going backward—

BROWN: Must I be the lady?

WARREN: —And the man forward, we make a box: 1, 2, 3, 4, 1, 2, 3, 4—

BROWN: *(Following awkwardly)* It's quite a simple one, isn't it?

WARREN: Four-four time, very easy. Are you enjoying it?

BROWN: It has a rhythm that's graspable.

WARREN: *(Pulling* BROWN *closer)* Much nicer than those decadent Viennese waltzes.

BROWN: Decadent, yes, indeed. Terrible.

WARREN: A clean American dance, for a clean, new American century.

BROWN: Clean, yes.

WARREN: *(Gropes* BROWN's *crotch)* Respectable. And yet romantic.

BROWN: Sir! *(Pulling away)*

WARREN: Stay in character, or I win!

BROWN: *(After a moment)* More romantic would be a kiss.

WARREN: A kiss?

BROWN: Before—anything else—

WARREN: *(Suddenly butch and hostile)* What makes you think I want a kiss?

BROWN: *(Losing camp)* Nothing, sir. Nothing at all. I have no interest in such things.

WARREN: Nor I. But how do you know Frederick Purssord?

BROWN: *(Suddenly detached)* I never knew him personally, but his degeneracy was featured in all the papers— "The most indecent man I ever met," said one of his neighbors.

WARREN: You read the papers, sir?

BROWN: It is my profession.

WARREN: A reporter?

BROWN: Yes, of vice. The things I've seen...!

WARREN: What are you doing?

BROWN: *(Dropping character)* Improvising!

WARREN: Who's this reporter?

BROWN: *(Vigorously shaking hands)* Fisher's the name, Eugene Fisher. With *The Sacramento Bee*. I'm here on special assignment.

WARREN: Attired thus?

BROWN: Catch up!

BROWN/FISHER: My paper's owner, Charles Kenny McClatchy, sent me undercover to uncover—

(With the addition of a hand prop or costume piece, perhaps a green eyeshade, BROWN turns WARREN into CHARLES KENNY MCCLATCHY. WARREN seems slightly stunned.)

BROWN/FISHER: Mister McClatchy, you sent me to uncover—

WARREN/MCCLATCHY: *(Coarse voice)* —A giant fucking scandal in Long Beach!

BROWN/FISHER: You were never so right, Mister McClatchy! There in Long Beach, the town touting itself as the religious capital of the West, depravity is growing and spreading like a hideous ulcer.

WARREN/MCCLATCHY: *(Overly delighted)* It is the way of the hypocrites: pray louder to drown out the wet and painful moans of lust!

BROWN/FISHER: At one unseemly gathering, a dinner party, next to everyone's plate perched a candy representation of a man's privates, which was sucked and enjoyed by each guest to the evident amusement of all.

WARREN/MCCLATCHY: Disgusting! More!

BROWN/FISHER: The Long Beach Police Department
has hired two actors to impersonate degenerates in
order to lure these lewd and dissolute persons into
revealing their perversities so they may be brought,
writhing, into the light of the law.

WARREN/MCCLATCHY: Surely that's on the Q T?

BROWN/FISHER: From the horse's mouth. I encountered
Mister Warren, one of the special officers, patrolling a
disreputable establishment.

WARREN/MCCLATCHY: Was it a sailor bar?

BROWN/FISHER: No...but Long Beach has many
of those, too. And sailors, used to life at sea in an
exclusive, masculine society, prefer the embrace—

WARREN/MCCLATCHY: —Or at least the mouth—

BROWN/FISHER & WARREN/ MCCLATCHEY: Of other
sailors!

BROWN: Are they our quarry, as you call them?

WARREN: No, it's easier than that. In a sailor bar, full of
men in navy, who stands out?

BROWN: The civilian male.

WARREN: Exactly! Mister Brown, you are a quick study!
If you are not a sailor—

BROWN: I'm not!

WARREN: If you are not a sailor, why patronize one of
these establishments?

BROWN: To meet sailors?

WARREN: Like a whore her trick. Our quarry is easily
spotted. Look, there's one now!

(When BROWN turns to look, WARREN adds a dandyish
costume piece, becomes HERBERT LOWE, 40, and steps in
front of BROWN.)

WARREN/LOWE: *(Minnesota accent)* Good evening.

(LOWE is more gentle than effeminate, dignified but easy-going.)

BROWN: *(Nervous)* Good evening.

WARREN/LOWE: You're not from Long Beach.

BROWN: My accent?

WARREN/LOWE: No, I just know everyone in Long Beach. *(Offers to shake hands)* Herbert Lowe.

BROWN: You're not from Long Beach either.

WARREN/LOWE: My accent? No, I'm from Lake City, Minnesota.

WARREN: *(Turning back to himself)* Good, good. Draw him out.

BROWN: Why are you here?

WARREN/LOWE: In this bar?

WARREN: *(Back to himself)* No, no! That's threatening! Too direct!

BROWN: Here in Long Beach. Why'd you leave Minnesota?

WARREN/LOWE: Family. We have a nursery business. In California we can go year-round.

BROWN: Cold in Minnesota.

WARREN/LOWE: Much warmer here.

WARREN: There's an opening. Carefully—!

BROWN: Warmer than Chicago, where I'm from.

WARREN/LOWE: Why are *you* here?

WARREN: He's probing *you*. Exactly what you want. Go a step farther.

BROWN: In this bar?

WARREN: Brilliant! Use his locutions!

WARREN/LOWE: In California.

BROWN: I'm an actor.

WARREN/LOWE: Ah, motion pictures. Might I have—?

BROWN: Not yet.

WARREN/LOWE: And your name, sir?

BROWN: Uh...Brown.

WARREN: Not your real name! Jesus!

BROWN: Jesus Brown.

WARREN: Oh, good God.

WARREN/LOWE: Is your mother Spanish?

WARREN: You have to go with it.

BROWN/JESUS: Yes, that's right. From Mexico.

WARREN/LOWE: May I call you— *(Pronounced in Spanish) Jesus*?

BROWN/JESUS: Of course. *(Quickly)* But I don't speak Spanish!

WARREN/LOWE: Your mother didn't want you to get an accent.

BROWN/JESUS: That's right. Very perceptive, Mister Lowe.

WARREN/LOWE: And please call me Herbert.

WARREN: He's getting personal. Take it further!

BROWN/JESUS: Did you happen to know Fred Prussord?

WARREN/LOWE: Purssord, and he always went by Frederick. Very formal fellow.

BROWN/JESUS: So you did know him?

WARREN/LOWE: Yes, why?

BROWN/JESUS: Terrible what happened to him.

WARREN/LOWE: Very intimate funeral. I donated the flowers, of course.

BROWN/JESUS: Really?

WARREN/LOWE: I'm a florist. And he was a friend. Don't know what's going to happen to all his businesses.

BROWN/JESUS: I was only aware of the Merced Hotel.

WARREN/LOWE: He had Turkish baths as well.

WARREN: Push him on that!

BROWN/JESUS: Were they nice?

WARREN/LOWE: They still are. I met Bothwell Browne at one of them.

BROWN/JESUS: At a Turkish bath? *(To* WARREN*)* Who the hell is that?

WARREN: Ask *him.*

BROWN/JESUS: I don't know Bothwell Browne.

WARREN/LOWE: You never saw him perform the suicide of Cleopatra?

BROWN/JESUS: *He* performs Cleopatra?

WARREN/LOWE: Why he's only the most daring female impersonator in the world. Not a hypocrite like Julian Eltinge running around punching anybody who calls him a fairy. Bothwell's Cleopatra made her encounter with the deadly asp a triumph of eroticism yet well within the bounds of tasteful entertainment.

BROWN/JESUS: The things you know, Mister Lowe!

WARREN/LOWE: *The Los Angeles Examiner* said, "Cleopatra, fondling the reptile, then holding it from her in horrible fascination of fear, determined upon death, finally crushes the venomed head to her bosom and expires in ecstatic agony!"

BROWN/JESUS: Oh, my! He's certainly no relation.

WARREN/LOWE: You've been missing out.

BROWN/JESUS: I don't think we have such people in Chicago.

WARREN/LOWE: Both Browne and Eltinge perform there.

BROWN/JESUS: I have heard of Julian Eltinge. He has a theatre named after him in New York. *(Leaning in, almost as if for a kiss)* But what of those Turkish baths?

WARREN: No, too obvious! Commiserate! He's about to confide in you, I'm sure.

BROWN: Maybe *you* should meet up with him!

WARREN: I think he likes your type.

BROWN: Pretty?

WARREN: He follows drag performers around the country. An easy catch, but he's slipping through your fingers.

BROWN: All you've been able catch so far is one newspaper reporter who was in fact trying to catch you!

WARREN: I've got one in the works, and Fisher's been a great help.

BROWN: How?

WARREN: First he sent us to Long Beach, then he sent me to church.

BROWN: Church?

WARREN: *(Putting FISHER's costume piece back on BROWN)* Right to the holy ones.

BROWN/FISHER: To the hypocrites!

WARREN: Which church?

BROWN/FISHER: Saint Luke's Episcopal. Got a lead on a Mister John Lamb, a druggist and a director at the Long Beach Savings Bank and Trust Company.

WARREN: Rich?

BROWN/FISHER: *(Nods)* But more importantly: prominent.

WARREN: *(Suspicious and perhaps envious)* Where do you get these leads?

BROWN/FISHER: A young man.

WARREN: Really, Mister Fisher?

BROWN/FISHER: L L Rollins. Brought up in Long Beach for social vagrancy a year ago, he seemed, well, lonely, and anxious to be of help.

(WARREN takes the cue and transforms, with the help of a costume piece, into ROLLINS.)

WARREN/ROLLINS: Oh, Mister Fisher, you wouldn't believe it! At this party—given by two Venice millionaires—really, millionaires!—

(WARREN/ROLLINS finds a kimono on the costume rack and shows it to BROWN/FISHER.)

WARREN/ROLLINS: —Each guest got a silk kimono, a wig and slippers. This was just before I got—you know—arrested. Fourteen of us chickens got invited cause they said we could meet some prominent queers. By the end of the night all manner of—I'll be delicate— unnatural practices were...practiced. Two of us got up in girl's clothes and entertained with music and song.

BROWN/FISHER: He's been invaluable.

WARREN: No doubt.

BROWN/FISHER: Apparently he had some kind of liaison with Mister Lamb, who later wanted nothing to do with him. I've been able to exploit Mister Rollin's injured dignity.

WARREN/ROLLINS: Seemed like a genuine fellow except for that English—Irish—Scotch—whatever-it-is accent which made him a trifle hard to fathom, if you know what I mean. But cut me off like I was some grasping doxy and turned out he ain't what he was cracked up to be.

BROWN/FISHER: Saint Luke's is at the corner of Locust and Fifth. Just listen for someone speaking Scottish.

(BROWN *puts on something vaguely Scottish. Probably not a kilt. But maybe. Or possibly just a fancy Sunday hat to show he's upper crust.*)

WARREN: Excuse me, I couldn't help but overhear your burr.

BROWN/LAMB: *(Scottish accent)* And who might you be, sir?

BROWN/FISHER: Use an accent on him, too. For sympathy.

WARREN: *(German accent)* Ach, one also new to America.

BROWN/LAMB: Not that new myself, sir. I came from Scotland in eighty-eight.

WARREN: Just don't believe it. You must have come as an infant!

BROWN/LAMB: *(Laughs)* You flatter me, sir. What's your name?

WARREN/LAMM: Johan Lamm.

BROWN/LAMB: What an extraordinary coincidence!

WARREN/LAMM: What is that?

BROWN/LAMB: My name's the same, but in English: John Lamb.

WARREN/LAMM: My twin! No, worse still—*mein Doppelganger!*

BROWN/LAMB: Astonished to make your acquaintance, Herr Lamm! *Guten morgen!*

WARREN/LAMM: *(Sotto voce)* Ach, *bitte*, not so loud. It's not a good year to be German in America.

BROWN/LAMB: Pardon me, Mister Lamm. I understand how an alien feels. After twelve years, I'm only beginning to feel part of Long Beach society.

WARREN/LAMM: But you are well regarded at Saint Luke's, on the vestry?

BROWN/LAMB: The Lord has been good to me. Tis only right I give back some of my blessings through service to God and man.

WARREN/LAMM: You are also quite generous to your maiden sister, if I am not mistaken.

BROWN/LAMB: You truly are my doppelganger, Johan Lamm. Is there anything about me you don't know?

WARREN/LAMM: I wish to know more about you, John Lamb, and about Long Beach. I haven't even been in the water yet!

BROWN/LAMB: Now's the only time to go, end of summer when the water's tolerable warm. Cold as bathing off the Orkneys the rest of the year!

WARREN/LAMM: What beach do you recommend, sir? Is there one with a public changing house?

BROWN/LAMB: *(Suddenly wary)* There is one, Mister Lamm, in Pacific Park.

WARREN/LAMM: Have you been there, Mister Lamb?

BROWN/LAMB: *(Intrigued but cautious)* On occasion, yes.

BROWN: *(Suddenly breaking character)* Mister Warren, I've grown increasingly uncomfortable with this scheme. It's all very well and good in the abstract, combatting vice and everything, but this Mister John Lamb seems a perfectly nice fellow, no caterwauling fairy.

WARREN: Mister Brown, your Herbert Lowe is no less likeable, yet you've no qualm leading him on.

BROWN: I do have qualms! That's my point!

WARREN: Why, you've a soft spot for Mister Lowe, haven't you?

BROWN: I do not!

WARREN: You've taken a shine to him!

BROWN: No, it's just not decent—deceiving such an honest and open gent—and Mister Lamb, too—

WARREN: You're falling in love with your own creation!

BROWN: Whatever do you mean?

WARREN: Your Mister Lamb is so well done, so effectively rendered in a few strokes, tender and vulnerable—

BROWN: I'm not in love with him, but it sounds like you are!

WARREN: I've given you but mannerisms, and you've swallowed them as truth, let your emotions run away with you! Where lie your loyalties, Mister Brown? With society or with—?

BROWN: I've gone this far with you—

WARREN: But not all the way—

BROWN: Be fair, sir—

WARREN: All's fair, Mister Brown. Just ask Mister Lowe.

BROWN: Ask him what?

WARREN: Ask him about love!

BROWN: Love?

WARREN: Probe his heart like a good Russian actor!

WARREN/LOWE: *(Suddenly* LOWE *again)* Love, *Jesus?* What a fraught topic!

BROWN/JESUS: Do you...believe in it, Mister Lowe?

WARREN/LOWE: Herbert!

BROWN/JESUS: Herbert. Do you...believe?

WARREN/LOWE: Well, we have to, don't we? Or what's the point of living? Nothing lasts, even mountains crumble to dust and some day the ocean will be a desert. And what we do in our lives, no matter how many stunning floral tributes I arrange, no matter how many motion pictures you star in, the flowers quickly wither and celluloid deterioriates—I've heard it can even spontaneously combust! So all we have is the moment, and the moment does not last. All we can do is fill that moment with love.

BROWN/JESUS: Mister Lowe—

BROWN/JESUS & WARREN/LOWE: Herbert!

BROWN/JESUS: I believe you are...quite correct.

WARREN/LOWE: So what can we do about that? In this moment?

WARREN: He's giving you the opening. Take it!

BROWN: What of your Mister Lamb? You seem a bit taken with him as well.

WARREN: Johan Lamm seems taken, without a doubt. Tis my job to act that part!

BROWN: You urge me to the game, but you're no closer to an arrest than I.

WARREN: I'll beat you to it, Mister Brown. I'm years ahead of you on the stage. Slink away—you've lost already!

BROWN: I'll bag my Lowe before you slaughter your Lamb!

WARREN: Do your best, sir!

BROWN/LAMB: You've not yet used our Long Beach public bathing house, Mister Lamm?

WARREN/LAMM: No, sir. Although I've heard a bit about it.

BROWN/LAMB: Have you, now?

WARREN/LOWE: *Jesus*, have you heard of the 96 Club?

BROWN/JESUS: No, what's that?

WARREN/LOWE: It's a safe place. A refuge, even, for, well, gentlemen such as ourselves, if I may presume.

BROWN/JESUS: You...may.

WARREN/LOWE: We need such sanctuaries, to let our hair down, so to speak. I don't believe in hiding, all of Long Beach knows who I am, but a florist must sell, and a salesman mustn't offend. On the street one must maintain one's—ambiguity—is probably the proper word. But in the 96 Club—you understand the name, don't you, a little joke?

BROWN/JESUS: Does it have to do with The Twentieth-Century Way?

WARREN/LOWE: *(Beaming)* Indeed, *Jesus*, indeed it does!

BROWN/FISHER: *The Sacramento Bee* is losing patience Mister Warren. Don't waste my lead!

WARREN: If I push, Mister Lamb will become suspicious. He's already wary.

BROWN/FISHER: Don't tempt me to doubt your skills, sir.

WARREN/LAMM: Would you take me to the bathing house sometime, Mister Lamb?

BROWN/LAMB: I can certainly give you directions. It's right—

WARREN/LAMM: No, no. *Take* me.

BROWN/JESUS: Herbert—

WARREN/LOWE: Yes?

BROWN/JESUS: We've only just met but you've already been kinder to me than anyone in California.

WARREN/LOWE: I know how it feels to be an outsider. Actors are always outsiders, aren't they?

BROWN/JESUS: I am so lonely sometimes, Herbert.

WARREN/LOWE: It's a lonely life, acting, because you are most yourself when playing someone else. No one gets to know you except through your characters, isn't that so?

BROWN/JESUS: I feel you've just revealed my character this very moment!

WARREN/LOWE: The real you! I am honored to know you, *Jesus*.

BROWN/JESUS: Then I hope you'll not be offended—

WARREN/LOWE: Never!

BROWN/JESUS: I've another favor to ask. I'll have to leave my rooming house soon—

WARREN/LOWE: Oh, *Jesus*, not another word! I've a guest cottage on my property standing vacant at this very moment!

WARREN/MCCLATCHY: Fisher! What's the pissant hesitation?

BROWN/FISHER: The hook is baited, sir.

WARREN/MCCLATCHY: Then where's your goddam report?

BROWN/FISHER: I sense...our agents confronting a moral ambiguity.

WARREN/MCCLATCHY: Ambiguity! Then pay them, goddamnit! That always eliminates ambiguity!

BROWN: Mister Warren, can you not sympathize with my uncertainty? Mister Lowe has been most generous with me, and I'm about to deal him an awful blow.

WARREN: This is your test, Mister Brown. And tests are built with such hurdles on purpose—to try your mettle! Don't trip over your heart!

BROWN: Surely this is life or death for Mister Lowe. Everything he has built, his business, his social standing—

WARREN: Tis life and death for us as well. Have you eaten today? I require the fifteen dollars per arrest! I need whatever Fisher will pay for the story! Is your situation less dire than mine?

BROWN: No. But morally—

WARREN: Morals are expensive—

BROWN: He keeps calling me Jesus!

WARREN: —And we cannot afford them, sir!

BROWN: Your Mister Lamb has more to lose than anyone. A churchman! Surely you sympathize with him!

WARREN: With a rich man?

BROWN: An arrest would kill him, as surely as starvation kills us, and quicker, too! Can you turn your back so cruelly on his kindness?

WARREN: Crumbs from his table!

BROWN/LAMB: Mister Lamm, you said you're an actor?

WARREN/LAMM: Yes, indeed Mister Lamb. Of stage in Germany and—*mit viel gluck!*—on the screen in America as well.

BROWN/LAMB: I know a few people in the industry.

WARREN/LAMM: You do, sir?

BROWN/LAMB: Not that I wish to presume—

WARREN/LAMM: No, no—I would be most grateful—

BROWN/LAMB: Introductions are easily made.

WARREN/LOWE: *(Overlapping)* Introductions are easily made. The 96 Club is more exclusive, more hermetic than the Elks, the Moose, the Masons. We meet in private homes, a different house each month. We are quiet, discreet, but not furtive! There's a strange and liberating joy in it!

WARREN: Ask him how many.

BROWN: How many what?

WARREN: How many members!

BROWN/JESUS: Is it a large club, Mister Lowe—?

BROWN/JESUS & WARREN/LOWE: Herbert!

WARREN/LOWE: There are no written rolls, for obvious reasons, but close to fifty come each evening, more than a hundred involved over the course of a year.

BROWN/JESUS: One hundred!

WARREN: Times fifteen—that's fifteen hundred dollars—within reach! He's just one cockroach, but don't stomp him till he leads you back to the nest! Get names!

BROWN: Mister Warren, this is quite enough. What an unsavory and unsatisfying enterprise! I've been here now a good three hours.

WARREN: Actors wait. That's our life.

BROWN: They're never going to audition either of us.

(WARREN *just grins.*)

BROWN: Your Chesshire grin is not a comfort, sir.

WARREN: This is it.

BROWN: This is what?

WARREN: This is your audition.

BROWN: Someone's watching us?

WARREN: I'm watching.

BROWN: You are?

WARREN: I'm with the motion picture company. I'm auditioning you.

BROWN: Is *this* how they audition in Hollywood?

WARREN: You're being judged on how you perform right now. Are you imaginative? Quick on your feet?

(BROWN *stares for a moment, then laughs in disbelief.*)

BROWN: You're trying to spoil my audition. You *want* me to leave so you can get the part!

WARREN: If you believe that, you're free to go.

BROWN: *(After a moment)* Or continue this charade? Bewildered by what you want, who you are? Not trusting—anyone, doubting reality itself?

WARREN: An actor's life.

BROWN: Never getting to be yourself.

WARREN: Everyone's life is improvisation, outward appearance. Who gets to be themselves, *really*? Leave the audition if you think it's wise, if you're not up to it. *(Shrugs)* Leave life.

(BROWN *starts to leave.*)

WARREN: But you've given a terrific performance thus far.

BROWN: I have?

WARREN: Not every actor improvises so inventively. Maybe there is something to be said for your method.

BROWN: Thank you.

WARREN: You very nearly have the part. Twould be a pity to lose out now. Impress me.

BROWN: Whyever should I wish to impress you?

WARREN: Perhaps you want more than just a part in a motion picture. Surely there's something else you desire, Mister Brown.

BROWN: What could I possibly desire so passionately?

WARREN: *(Smiles)* To beat me.

BROWN/FISHER: *(After a moment)* We have our story, Mister McClatchy!

WARREN/MCCLATCHY: Our boys come through?

BROWN/FISHER: They've been heroic, sir.

WARREN/MCCLATCHY: Gotta love those sons of bitches!

BROWN/FISHER: *(Reading from notes)* None of this is announced yet—I've got an exclusive on it so far, but they're panting to go to the *L A Times*—

WARREN/MCCLATCHY: Pay the fuckers!

BROWN/FISHER: The activities of Special Vice Officers Warren and Brown have thus far resulted in sixteen arrests, most at the public bathing house in Long Beach. Brown and Warren take turns loitering in the changing area and toilet stalls, many with walls already perforated for immoral purposes—

WARREN/MCCLATCHY: What a foul practice!

BROWN/FISHER: When they spy a gentleman given to such things—and they've become quite expert at it, I must say—one of them sits in an adjacent stall and puts a finger through the hole—

WARREN/MCCLATCHY: Glory holes, they call 'em.

BROWN/FISHER: Yes, glory holes, I believe they do. This garners the attention of the fellow next door, and if he peers through the hole he will see an open mouth, waiting—

WARREN/MCCLATCHY: I'm nauseated, please proceed.

BROWN/FISHER: The gentleman then, more often than not, puts his erect penis through the hole—

WARREN/MCCLATCHY: Dear God, Fisher, we can't say penis in *The Sacramento Bee*!

BROWN/FISHER: These are just my notes, sir, not a finished story—

WARREN/MCCLATCHY: And what of the churchgoers? The pious hypocrites of Long Beach? That's the real story, Fisher! Garden variety queers poking their dicks through toilet partitions—we've got them aplenty here in Sacramento!

BROWN/FISHER: I'm getting to that, Mister McClatchy.

WARREN/MCCLATCHY: I want an arrest with controversy! Someone with social standing!

BROWN/FISHER: Mister Brown has been invited to a meeting of the 96 Club, a private gathering of the well-to-do—

WARREN/MCCLATCHY: That's more like it, Fisher. When is Brown attending this debauch?

BROWN: I'm not going.

WARREN: What?

BROWN: Our purpose is to raid the party and arrest all present, yes?

WARREN: Just as we've done in toilet after toilet, Mister Brown.

BROWN: With strangers! Men I only know—God help me—by their—members! Not even by face!

WARREN: This will be even easier. You'll see their faces.

BROWN: I'll meet them. Have conversations. Smile and laugh. Then clamp handcuffs on 'em!

WARREN: Do you feel it's rude?

BROWN: I can't.

WARREN: Mister Brown, you've done outstanding groundwork, detective work, really, getting the invitation and address to the party. Your cockroach has led us to the nest!

BROWN: That's just it. Herbert will be there.

WARREN: And you can't—?

BROWN: *(Overlapping)* I can't arrest him.

WARREN: Then I'll do it.

BROWN: Good. You go.

WARREN: You have to go, too!

BROWN: He said I could bring a friend if I wanted. Just tell him I sent you.

WARREN: He'll be suspicious!

BROWN: Surely, Mister Warren, you have sufficient skill to put him at ease.

WARREN: Don't be a pussy!

BROWN: Are you afraid to go without me? Are your emotions getting the better of *you*? So far we've nabbed these fellows one-by-one in public. Is the idea of an entire house crawling with them too much for you?

WARREN: You little shit.

BROWN: You don't want the address?

WARREN: Give it to me.

BROWN: I wouldn't want you to feel uncomfortable.

WARREN: Shut up, you ninny!

(BROWN *shuts up. After a moment*)

WARREN: And give me the address.

BROWN: Number 1406 Alamitos Avenue. (*He goes to the rack to get costume changes.*)

WARREN: Number 1406 Alamitos Avenue.

(BROWN *transforms into* ALBERT, *the party host. Slight Scandinavian accent*)

BROWN/ALBERT: Hello.

WARREN/LAMM: My name is Johan Lamm.

BROWN/ALBERT: Are you a spy?

WARREN/LAMM: I beg your pardon?

BROWN/ALBERT: A German spy? (*Laughs*) Just joking, Mister Lamm. But this is a private party.

WARREN/LAMM: Jesus Brown sent me. He's a friend of Herbert Lowe.

BROWN/ALBERT: Oh, Herbie, ja sure! Come on in. Welcome to the 96 Club! I'm Albert—let me introduce you round—

WARREN/LAMM: (*Shaking* BROWN/ALBERT's *hand*) Pleasure.

BROWN/ALBERT: This is Roy.

WARREN/LAMM: Very nice to meet you, sir.

BROWN/ROY: (*Southern accent.*) Now, Johan, we're dispensing with such formality this evening! Are you new to Long Beach? Haven't seen you at the 96 Club afore this.

WARREN/LAMM: Ja, I am new. To this country a little bit as well!

BROWN/ROY: You're gonna love it, son. California can't be beat. You meet the nicest folks.

(BROWN *quickly becomes* ALBERT *again.*)

BROWN/ALBERT: Nice folks such as Aref, also new to America! He is from Turkey.

WARREN/LAMM: You don't say!

(BROWN *turns into* AREF, *who brings a kimono and puts it on* WARREN.)

BROWN/AREF: You must dress proper, Johan. No need for face paint, though, for you are pretty enough already.

WARREN/LAMM: *(Almost breaking character)* Pretty!?

BROWN/AREF: *(Giggles)* Pretty sensitive! You'll fit right in! George, come meet Johan. I think he is just your type—excitable and German!

WARREN/LAMM: But I am American now! Might even enlist in the army!

(BROWN *dons his own kimono to become* GEORGE.)

BROWN/GEORGE: Oooo! *(With a major lisp or sibilance)* A soldier boy! Fascinating! I don't suppose you could do a Prussian goosestep for me? *(Goosesteps awkwardly in his kimono.)*

WARREN/LAMM: Is Herbert Lowe here yet?

BROWN/GEORGE: She's always late, the socialite biddy! But don't worry, she wouldn't miss you for the world! I'm sure she's looking forward to it.

WARREN/LAMM: I am looking forward to some sucking and fucking!

BROWN/GEORGE: Sucking and fucking! Johan, you are certainly direct. A man after my own heart. But first a little song and dance, some wine, or maybe something stronger! *(He gets out of the kimono.)*

BROWN/JOSEPH: *(Italian accent)* Now, Georgie, leave-a him alone. You gotta grab alla the nice boys fora youself?

WARREN/LAMM: I can't wait much longer for Mister Lowe.

BROWN/ALBERT: *(Handing WARREN a drink)* Don't you worry, Johan, Herbie almost always makes it eventually.

WARREN/LAMM: I came specifically to meet him.

BROWN/AREF: Oh, you're not a friend of his?

WARREN/LAMM: No, a friend of a friend. Jesus Brown.

BROWN/ROY: Who's that, now? Jesus Brown? Do we know him?

WARREN/LAMM: I don't think so. He was going to meet me here tonight as well.

BROWN/ROY: Awful lot of strangers this evening.

WARREN/LAMM: No, just me. Jesus said he might not make it anyways.

(BROWN transforms into a new party guest, C C.)

BROWN/C C: *(New York accent just like WARREN's own)* He's gonna meet you, but now he might not make it?

WARREN/LAMM: Ja, that's perfectly understandable, isn't it? Silly little queen. Flighty, you know!

BROWN/C C: And who names their kid Jesus?

WARREN/LAMM: It's Spanish, I think. *(Spanish pronunciation)* Hay-zoos.

44 THE TWENTIETH–CENTURY WAY

BROWN/ROY: Sounds kinda made-up to me. Like a fake name.

BROWN/ALBERT: We've all used fake names now and again, Roy!

BROWN/C C: But not at the 96 Club. And there's something funny about your accent, Johan. *Sprechen zie Deutsch?*

WARREN/LAMM: *Ja, ja!*

BROWN/C C: Me, too. My ma came from Silesia, near Poland. *Wer sind Sie wirklich?* [Who are you really?]

WARREN/LAMM: I am sorry, sir, I think your dialect is not—

BROWN/C C: It's High German, Herr Lamm. Ma was very proud of that.

WARREN/LAMM: Then perhaps your accent—?

BROWN/C C: Your accent's the one in question—

WARREN/LAMM: Perhaps I've been in America too long—

BROWN/ALBERT: C C, that's not very hospitable!

WARREN/LAMM: I forget my German, maybe!

BROWN/JOSEPH: Have you done-a something with Herbie? Why'sa he not here-a!

WARREN/LAMM: Gentlemen, please! I was told the 96 Club welcomed the stranger!

BROWN/AREF: Impostor! Impostor! Throw him out!

BROWN/GEORGE: *(Wildly sibilant or lisping)* There's something suspicious about you, sir!

(Panicked, WARREN pulls out a police whistle and blows it. BROWN dashes about, simulating the party-goers fleeing a police raid all by himself.)

BROWN/ALBERT: Everybody out! Back door! Back door!

WARREN: Come and get 'em boys!

BROWN/C C: I told you—that bastard!

WARREN: Round 'em up! They've been talking that fairy talk all night.

BROWN/ROY: It's always the cute ones betray you!

(Taking off the kimono, WARREN makes the sound of a police siren.)

BROWN/AREF: *(Grabbing a kimono)* I spent a fortune on these kimonos! They're real silk!

BROWN/JOSEPH: Drop-a that, Aref, and run! Here-a they come-a!

BROWN/GEORGE: Get your hands off me, motherfucker! I am fierce! Fear me!

WARREN: Get that one in the Japanesy dress-thing!

BROWN/ALBERT: Officer, this is my house. Do you have a warrant?

(WARREN pulls out handcuffs.)

WARREN: This party's over, fellows!

BROWN/C C: You son of a bitch!

WARREN: You're under arrest, pansy!

BROWN/ROY: You can't arrest me! Who the hell are you?

(WARREN puts BROWN/ROY in handcuffs.)

WARREN: I'm Special Vice Officer Warren of the Long Beach Police Department!

BROWN/ROY: You tricked us! You lied!

WARREN: I only lied to expose the truth. The hideous truth!

(BROWN and WARREN stand there a moment, catching their breath.)

BROWN: You can...take these off now.

WARREN: Maybe I should leave 'em on a bit. Show you who's boss.

BROWN: You always bring handcuffs to auditions?

WARREN: I bring 'em everywhere.

BROWN: Too bad you don't speak German.

WARREN: And since when do you?

BROWN: My ma's from Silesia.

WARREN: Really?

BROWN: Use what you got, like you said. Now take these off.

WARREN: What we didn't get was Herbert Lowe.

BROWN: Can I help it he didn't show?

WARREN: I don't know. Can you?

BROWN: What do you mean?

WARREN: Did you help it? Help him? Warn him not to go?

BROWN: No, you're crazy. Most likely he just got suspicious.

WARREN: Don't hold out on me.

BROWN: I'm not.

WARREN: This might not be an audition.

BROWN: What?

WARREN: This might be an arrest. A real one.

BROWN: *(Frightened)* Who the fuck are you? I mean it— tell me!

(WARREN *just stares, smiling.*)

BROWN: I'm not holding out on you! Take 'em off!

(WARREN *unlocks the handcuffs.*)

WARREN: You held out on the German.

BROWN: Keeping you on your toes.

WARREN: For that I'm making you nab Lowe on your own.

BROWN: You think I can't?

WARREN: Not long ago you were whining about betrayal.

BROWN: I never used that word. I'll nab Lowe after you nab Lamb.

WARREN: No, huh-uh.

BROWN: You been putting it off.

WARREN: Not true.

BROWN: You're uncomfortable with it, I can tell. Betrayal—your word. Maybe you're a nicer fellow than you make out to be.

WARREN: It's a job!

BROWN: Then do it.

WARREN: All right. But it's a dirty job. And you're the one afraid of getting your hands dirty, Mister Brown.

BROWN: Afraid?!

WARREN/LAMM: Beautiful day!

BROWN: What?

WARREN/LAMM: Beautiful September day for a swim, Mister Lamb.

BROWN/LAMB: Please call me John.

WARREN/LAMM: Thanks for bringing me to the bathing house, John. Do we change into swimming attire in these stalls?

BROWN/LAMB: That's correct, Johan. See how progressive we are in Long Beach?

WARREN/LAMM: Will the water be terribly cold?

BROWN/LAMB: It's never tropical—think of it as invigorating.

WARREN/LAMM: The temperature change might shock my system. I believe I'll relieve myself first.

BROWN/LAMB: Excellent thought, Johan. I'll do the same.

(They move chairs to either side of an empty section of the costume rack, creating toilet stalls. They may pull down their pants to sit on the toilets.)

BROWN/LAMB: *Kälte ist gesund!*

WARREN/LAMM: I beg your pardon?

BROWN/LAMB: Cold is healthy! Did I say it proper?

WARREN/LAMM: *Ja, ja. Kälte ist gesund!* Cold is indeed healthy!

(WARREN/LAMM is touching himself. BROWN/LAMB may do the same.)

BROWN/LAMB: And health is important.

WARREN/LAMM: I can tell you understand health, John.

BROWN/LAMB: I exercise a bit. Swimming keeps me vigorous.

(WARREN puts his finger through an imaginary hole between the stalls. BROWN/LAMB notices.)

WARREN/LAMM: Indeed.

BROWN/LAMB: You are a healthy young man as well, Johan, but too thin. I hope I'm not being too personal—

WARREN/LAMM: Not at all, John.

BROWN/LAMB: Permit me to take you to a marvelous place, the best beefsteak you'll ever taste—

WARREN/LAMM: You whet my appetite, John. I'm not worthy of it—

BROWN/LAMB: You mustn't think so little of yourself, Johan. You're a good man, deserving—

WARREN/LAMM: Actors are not always highly regarded.

(BROWN/LAMB *leans forward to peer in the "hole".* WARREN/LAMM *leans forward, positioning his open mouth near the hole so* BROWN/LAMB *sees it.* BROWN/LAMB *sits back, excited and nervous.*)

BROWN/LAMB: What has been your favorite role?

WARREN/LAMM: In Germany we love Shakespeare.

(BROWN/LAMB *maneuvers cautiously toward the hole, trying to decide whether to put his penis through it.*)

BROWN/LAMB: In Scotland we enjoy *Macbeth.*

WARREN/LAMM: Ach! You mustn't speak the name out loud, John.

(*Sensing* BROWN/LAMB's *hesitation,* WARREN/LAMM *puts his finger through the hole again.*)

BROWN/LAMB: I thought that was just in theaters.

WARREN/LAMM: There are some things you should never speak at all.

(BROWN/LAMB *puts his penis through the hole.*)

BROWN/LAMB: Don't I know it, Johan! Some things not spoken are simply understood.

(WARREN/LAMM *takes out his black marking pen, hesitates.* BROWN/LAMB *starts getting nervous with his dick through a glory hole not getting sucked immediately as expected.*)

BROWN/LAMB: Isn't that so, Johan? (*No response*) Johan?

(BROWN/LAMB *starts to withdraw his penis, but* WARREN/LAMM *quickly grabs it.* BROWN/LAMB *relaxes in relief: his offer has been accepted.*)

WARREN/LAMM: That's so, John. Nothing could be truer.

(WARREN/LAMM *quickly makes a mark on* BROWN/LAMB's *penis.*)

BROWN/LAMB: Johan, what—?

WARREN: *(Dropping* LAMM's *accent)* Mister John Lamb—

(BROWN/LAMB *pulls away from the hole.*)

BROWN/LAMB: What have you done?

WARREN: —Of Long Beach, California—

WARREN: You're under arrest!

(*In a panic,* BROWN/LAMB *pulls up his pants and dashes out of the stall.*)

BROWN/LAMB: You bastard! Deceiver!

(*While* BROWN/LAMB *dashes about,* WARREN *remains in the stall, calmly adjusting his clothes.*)

WARREN: You can't escape, Mister Lamb. As fast as you may sprint through Pacific Park, my fellow officers will hunt you down. And the mark of your guilt is indelible, the mark of Cain, the mark of the beast. You've been acting as much as I, Mister Lamb, all meek and mild, when you're in fact a wolf, a predator, a ravenous despoiler of nature. But all predators may be baited and trapped—by their appetites.

(WARREN *steps out of the stall and easily captures the now thoroughly disheveled* BROWN/LAMB.)

BROWN/LAMB: Let me go, Johan. For the love of God!

(WARREN *puts the handcuffs on* BROWN/LAMB.)

WARREN: Invoking God, are you, my Scottish hypocrite? He won't hear your plea—tell it to the judge.

BROWN/LAMB: Johan, please!

WARREN: Johan's but an alias, sir, to play upon your perverse vanity. To lure you into fucking yourself.

BROWN/LAMB: You're destroying me, is what you're doing.

WARREN: I'm destroying vice, is all, and that's what you represent.

BROWN/LAMB: You—represent—too! I know who you are. We're the same! We're the same man!

WARREN: *(Positioning* BROWN/LAMB *with his back to the audience)* We're no such thing, sir. *(To an imaginary policeman)* Caught another fairy with his pants down, Officer Cervantes.

(Stepping to the other side of BROWN/LAMB, WARREN *becomes* CERVANTES, *perhaps with the addition of the police cap.)*

WARREN/CERVANTES: *(Spanish accent)* Where do you dig 'em up?

WARREN: *(Stepping back to the other side)* The comfort station in Pacific Park is rife with 'em. A gold mine of depravity.

WARREN/CERVANTES: *(Stepping to the other side)* Let's see the evidence.

*(*WARREN *fumbles with* BROWN/LAMB's *pants.)*

BROWN/LAMB: No, officers, please. This is a mistake. I never went to that park.

WARREN: Behold!

*(*WARREN *rips* BROWN/LAMB's *pants and underwear down to his knees, leaving* BROWN/LAMB *facing upstage, bare-assed and shivering.)*

WARREN/CERVANTES: *(Inspecting)* Sure enough. There's the black cross.

WARREN: It's not a cross—it's an X.

WARREN/CERVANTES: Cross, X, same thing.

WARREN: The cross has entirely different symbolism, Officer Cervantes. An X is a deletion, an erasure, a correction.

WARREN/CERVANTES: Well, I can hardly see it he's so shrunk with cold.

WARREN: *(Recalling* LAMM*) Kälte ist gesund,* Officer Cervantes, cold is healthy. I think it's fear that's shrunk him up. Look, the reprobate's in tears.

BROWN/LAMB: *(Crying)* I beg of you—! I never—!

WARREN: You begged me in the bathing house, Mister Lamb, but you'll not see me on my knees.

BROWN/LAMB: I pray God shows you the mercy you've not shown me, Mister Warren.

WARREN: What? I never told you my real—

*(*BROWN *suddenly becomes himself again.)*

BROWN: Well done, Mister Warren.

WARREN: Thank you kindly, Mister Brown.

*(*BROWN *proffers handcuffs for* WARREN *to release him.)*

BROWN: You humiliated him, stripped him, smote him.

*(*WARREN *ignores the handcuffs, instead pulling up and fastening* BROWN's *trousers. Slowly)*

WARREN: I smote him right proper. Twas very nearly Biblical.

BROWN: The Lamb went uncomplaining forth.

WARREN: Oh, he complained plenty.

BROWN: And what are your feelings, Mister Warren?

WARREN: My feelings? Incidental!

BROWN: Not at all. You're an actor. Emotions are your meat, empathy your bread and butter.

WARREN: *(Laughs dismissively)* What of *your* feelings, Mister Brown?

BROWN: I wasn't present for the arrest.

(Trying to squirm away as WARREN *dresses him.)*

BROWN: Now, if you'd kindly—

WARREN: But now you're in the limelight. I butchered my Lamb. Tis time to harvest your nurseryman.

BROWN: I'm observing him at close quarters from his guest cottage.

WARREN: What observation is necessary? The man's a deviate. Reel him in.

BROWN: I'm not so cold-hearted as you. Or at least as you pretend to be.

WARREN: Mister Brown, I'm winning our contest.

*(*BROWN *begins to display annoyance with* WARREN's *attentions.)*

BROWN: Which contest?

WARREN: Any time two men meet, it's a contest. You lag by one upper crust pansy. Can you even the score?

BROWN: Perhaps if you'd unlock these goddamn handcuffs!

WARREN: *(Removing the handcuffs)* Certainly, Mister Brown. I'm all for a fair fight.

BROWN: I may lack the talent.

WARREN: Nonsense. You've demonstrated great skill at mimicry. If your portrayal lacks depth, it's only because you've not yet achieved your climax. Your emotional climax.

BROWN: I don't feel like myself.

WARREN: Then you've truly assumed the role. The outer has transformed the inner.

BROWN: This isn't about acting!

WARREN: Everything is about acting.

BROWN: Not for normal people.

WARREN: For everyone. Your naivete astounds. Everyone's acting *all the time*. Every job is a role. Every relationship a masquerade.

BROWN: Can't we strip away the mask to reveal the truth?

WARREN: The naked truth—as we've seen—is often unpleasant. You'll find Herbert Lowe's a man like any other.

BROWN: I...can't.

WARREN: Your assignment just got easier. Thanks to the raid on the 96 Club, your Mister Lowe will be brimming with trepidation.

BROWN: Making my task all the harder.

WARREN: Now you have a new ally—fear. In his mind, *mutual* fear, for you assured him you were a gentleman like himself. Twine your souls. Mimic his affectations. Get him to tell you he loves you—then you've won.

BROWN: Or a kiss.

WARREN: Either way—evidence.

BROWN: Truth.

WARREN: Chief Cole and I will hide ourselves in the attic and outside the window so you won't be compromised.

BROWN: I don't feel—

WARREN/LOWE: Good evening, *Jesus*.

BROWN: I'm not ready!

WARREN/LOWE: Ready for what?

BROWN: Herbert, you startled me!

WARREN/LOWE: My apologies. I imagine you're jumpy, too, these days.

BROWN/JESUS: Twas fortunate we missed the 96 Club meeting.

WARREN/LOWE: I wish I'd been there. I dare them to arrest me.

BROWN/JESUS: You're not trepidatious?

WARREN/LOWE: I'm sensibly wary, no more. What are you reading?

BROWN/JESUS: Shakespeare.

WARREN/LOWE: Which play?

BROWN/JESUS: *Macbeth.*

WARREN/LOWE: Oh, that's a disturbing one, isn't it? *(Sits down next to* BROWN/JESUS*)* May I?

*(*BROWN/JESUS *nods.)*

WARREN/LOWE: So awful how hospitality is repaid with betrayal, affection with deception, all in the name of ambition. I played Duncan in college.

BROWN/JESUS: You were an actor?

WARREN/LOWE: We're all actors in our youth. Seeking the role we'll play the rest of our lives. I'm sorry—that was awfully pretentious!

BROWN/JESUS: Not nearly as pretentious as my friend.

WARREN/LOWE: Your friend?

BROWN/JESUS: An actor friend.

WARREN/LOWE: Ah.

BROWN/JESUS: Do you like your...role, Herbert?

WARREN/LOWE: My role in life? I certainly do. I live well within limits. When you're my age, you will, too.

BROWN/JESUS: I'm not a kid!

WARREN/LOWE: But younger than I.

BROWN/JESUS: I guess. And you're right—there's so much I don't know.

WARREN/LOWE: What luck! I'm a frustrated Socrates. How may I inculcate you?

BROWN/JESUS: Well, except on stage, I've never kissed anyone in my life.

WARREN/LOWE: Surely not!

BROWN/JESUS: Not everyone likes it.

WARREN/LOWE: Who doesn't like kissing?

BROWN/JESUS: My actor friend.

WARREN/LOWE: Perhaps he only acts like he doesn't like it.

BROWN/JESUS: That is his job. In more ways than one.

WARREN/LOWE: Kissing reveals the soul. Utter vulnerability. I adore it.

BROWN/JESUS: Really? You like being revealed?

WARREN/LOWE: *(Nods)* I'm a dreadful actor. I blush, I blanch—you can read my soul in my face. Study me and you can ignore everything Mister Stanislavsky says!

BROWN/JESUS: Me, too. I mean, I can't help but show how I feel. It just bursts out. I get embarrassed.

WARREN/LOWE: *(Hand on* BROWN/JESUS's *shoulder)* No need for embarrassment here.

BROWN/JESUS: It's...a refuge.

WARREN/LOWE: *(Taking his hand away)* That's right. Our private sanctuary.

BROWN/JESUS: *(Putting his hand on* WARREN/LOWE's *thigh.)* I never realized—until today...this is the role I've been seeking. I want to *act it.*

WARREN/LOWE: Then you must audition without delay.

(They lean in for a kiss. WARREN/LOWE *kicks the chair or makes some other kind of noise.)*

WARREN/LOWE: What was that?

BROWN/JESUS: I'll see.

WARREN/LOWE: Someone's in the attic!

*(*BROWN/JESUS *gets up, steps away, grabs the police cap and turns back to* WARREN/LOWE *as* COLE.*)*

BROWN/COLE: Mister Herbert Lowe, you're under arrest for social vagrancy.

WARREN/LOWE: Who are you? What are you doing on my property?

BROWN/COLE: My name's Cole. I'm the Chief of Police in Long Beach.

WARREN/LOWE: You can't just burst in here! What've you done with my tenant?!

BROWN/COLE: Don't worry about Brown, Mister Lowe. You're the one going to jail.

WARREN/LOWE: For what, sir? What is social vagrancy?

BROWN/COLE: I know it when I see it. And looking in your window I just saw it.

WARREN/LOWE: You saw nothing, sir. As a citizen of Long Beach I pay your salary, and I won't be intimidated!

BROWN/COLE: I don't care whether you're intimidated—you're arrested.

(WARREN *abandons his* LOWE *impersonation and whips the police cap from* BROWN's *head.*)

WARREN: Success, Mister Brown!

BROWN: Congratulations, Mister Warren.

WARREN: No, no—Herbert Lowe was your collar, not mine. In fact, I very nearly scotched our chances when I slipped in the attic and made a noise.

BROWN: Was that what I heard? At the critical moment, you slipped?

WARREN: Fascinated by your compelling performance, I leaned too close to the spy hole and overbalanced.

BROWN: Twas not a slip out of jealousy?

WARREN: Jealousy?

BROWN: As Lowe leaned in for a kiss?

WARREN: I fail to understand you, sir. Do you mean envy of your acting?

BROWN: Or was it simply fear? Of the naked truth?

WARREN: Enough of this nonsense, Mister Brown. We must prepare for the trial.

BROWN: As you wish, Mister Warren. But I admire Herbert for fighting the charge instead of paying a fine or going to jail like all the rest.

WARREN: Admire him? Now you've surely taken empathy too far.

BROWN: Must we proceed with prosecution?

WARREN: Tis no longer within our hands. The public demands our appearance upon the stage. Have you never had your name in the newspaper?

BROWN: Not yet.

WARREN: Now's your chance! We'll be called as witnesses for certain.

BROWN: I'll have to testify against Herbert?

WARREN: Twill be the performance of a lifetime.

BROWN: Mister Warren, our little improvisation
has mushroomed into madness, the whole town's
hysterical, and your only thought is publicity?

WARREN: I'm an actor.

BROWN: Surely actors care for their fellow man.

(WARREN *can't answer.*)

BROWN: At least a little? No empathy at all?

WARREN: Only as required to play the scene.

BROWN: Well played, my friend. Your Herbert Lowe
is your finest work—such heart, such *joi de vivre,* such
kindness. I envy *your* acting. Looking into Lowe's eyes
I saw your beautiful, frightened soul.

WARREN: You saw no such thing!

BROWN: Then who are you, Mister Warren? Truly?

(BROWN *waits for an answer.* WARREN *can't respond.*)

BROWN: Nothing but a soulless imitator of a human
being?

WARREN: I've told you—

BROWN: You've told me lies. It takes little
investigation—

WARREN: My dear Mister Brown—you are obsessed
with me!

BROWN: —To reveal you never reported for *The New
York Times,* your Brooklyn accent's as fraudulent as
your German—

WARREN: That's very funny as I was born in Flatbush—

BROWN: Even your name is a fabrication!

WARREN: Of course it is! I'd never get a job as Menachem Mendel Schneerson!

BROWN: That's your real name?

WARREN: No, just an example. Thaksin Shinawatra.

BROWN: You don't look Japanese.

WARREN: But I can *play* Japanese! Or Siamese! I'm an actor! Why should my real name matter?

BROWN: It matters to me.

WARREN: Only my roles matter. I don't exist. I'm born in the mind of the audience.

BROWN: And I'm your audience. I see you.

WARREN: Strip away my mask and you'll see nothing. Pour over the U S census record—you will not find me.

BROWN: What role will you play on the witness stand?

WARREN: Special Vice Officer Warren.

BROWN: You'll be perjuring yourself the moment you state your name.

WARREN: No, I'll be playing the role of the person perjuring himself.

BROWN: Why, Mister Warren, you've just declared yourself exempt from life!

(*Without warning,* WARREN *becomes the Long Beach Deputy District Attorney* ONG *and pushes* BROWN *into the witness chair.*)

WARREN/ONG: Special Vice Officer Brown, describe for me your relationship with Mister Herbert N Lowe.

BROWN: Our relationship?

WARREN/ONG: You are under oath, Officer Brown. And as Deputy District Attorney I'm cordially requesting the truth.

BROWN: I knew that Lowe had a house to rent in the rear of his residence at the corner of Broadway and Junipero streets. With the connivance of the Police Chief I rented his cottage.

WARREN/ONG: When Mister Lowe visited you on the evening of September 26 were there any officers present?

BROWN: Yes, I put Warren in the attic before Lowe came in, while I read a book. Chief Cole was hidden outside the window.

WARREN/ONG: What book?

BROWN: *(After a puzzled moment)* Shakespeare.

WARREN/ONG: What happened when Lowe arrived?

BROWN: He came in about eight o'clock, asked me how my bathing suit fit, and began to get familiar, as usual.

WARREN/ONG: And what did you do all this time?

BROWN: I did not like it, and, moving a little farther away, kept on reading my magazine.

WARREN/ONG: Book.

BROWN: Yes, Shakespeare, sorry.

WARREN: Well, that was terrible.

BROWN: It's what we rehearsed—

WARREN: Book? Magazine? Fucking Shakespeare?

BROWN: That part was true. It was *Macbeth*—

WARREN: What good is the truth if it's not convincing?

BROWN: Now there's a philosophy for the twentieth century! Perjury isn't a role I'm familiar with!

WARREN: Doesn't matter.

BROWN: Why not?

WARREN: *(Produces a newspaper)* We're famous.

BROWN: *(Grabbing the paper)* Let me see!

WARREN: *Los Angeles Times*, November 13, 1914—your first review!

BROWN: *(Reading)* The reports of Special Officers Warren and Brown and Judge Hart reveal a surprising array of convictions and fines of citizens on the same "social vagrancy" charge. Two prominent church men, John E Lamb and J A Hoyden, were fined five hundred dollars each. Other men who paid fines ranging from one hundred to two hundred dollars were: C C Espey, L E Arnold, J F Storey—

WARREN: We've got it made, Mister Brown! As actors, as vice officers! Everybody knows our names! After we're done with Long Beach, we'll be in great demand all up and down the coast! And studios who never gave us a second thought will be calling us in again and again. Bet we won't even have to audition! Notoriety at last!

BROWN: *(Overlapping)* —W S Austin, John Lain, Joseph Carrao, George Grimes, Roy Lyburger, Aref Said, Albert Leidstrom, and W J McCandless. Those who received six months' sentences in the County Jail are: Arthur Clarke, Robert Forbes, C F Edwards, P L Flaherty, W L Mead, Nels Berglund, H C Kerlin, George Grahm, W R Berry and Fred Long. Many people think political vengeance is at the bottom of it. But what a holy city Long Beach is!

WARREN/MCCLATCHY: Goddamnit, Mister Fisher! The *L A Times* scooped us! You've been following this story for months! How'd they get in ahead of us?!

BROWN/FISHER: We'll do a feature, Mister McClatchy, an in-depth article—a series! No one has more notes—

WARREN/MCCLATCHY: Notes mean crap unless they turn into stories! Get back down to Los Angeles

and stick to the case like shit on a shoe! Play up
the religious angle! How's Long Beach liking its
churchmen now?

BROWN/LAMB: My darling sister: God knows, and will
have mercy through Christ. I am crazed by reading the
paper this morning. I never knew of such a place or of
such orgies. I am innocent, but the victim of a situation.
I could not endure this publicity as I had not a chance
to deny it. Go to the office and Mister Tucker will act
as your advisor. The Third Street property is yours by
deed. Have it recorded. How I love you, but it is best.
Be brave. Believe me innocent. John.

(WARREN *turns into* LOWE *in conversation with his
attorney,* ROLAND SWAFFIELD.)

WARREN/LOWE: Mister Swaffield, your legal expertise
notwithstanding, I'm a florist!

BROWN/SWAFFIELD: *(Michigan accent)* That doesn't
mean you're guilty. As your attorney, I must remind
you that you never confessed.

WARREN/LOWE: Not guilty, not of what they say. All
that talk of his bathing costume! I never pulled back
any blankets or kissed him all over. They arrested me
before anything happened!

BROWN/SWAFFIELD: But he asked you to kiss him?

WARREN/LOWE: Must I speak of that?

BROWN/SWAFFIELD: So we can discredit the witness.

WARREN/LOWE: He said he'd never kissed anyone
before.

BROWN/SWAFFIELD: He wanted that kiss as much as
you did!

WARREN/LOWE: But I am...what they say I am.
Everyone in Long Beach knows it's true.

BROWN/SWAFFIELD: You can't be tried for being something, only for doing something.

WARREN/LOWE: Would that that were true.

BROWN/SWAFFIELD: We'll change the world and make it true.

BROWN: *(Glancing at the newspaper in his hand)* Oh, my God.

WARREN: What?

BROWN: *(Reading the newspaper)* John A Lamb, banker and prominent churchman, ended his life this morning on the rocks near Point Fermin, as a result of the expose of a clique of "social vagrants" that has shaken this city to its very foundations.

(BROWN hands the paper to WARREN who continues reading.)

WARREN: *(Reading)* The body of Lamb was found on the rocky beach at a point about half a mile east of Point Fermin by Mrs F E Grossley and sister, Mrs Dunbar. Horrified by their find, and recognizing Lamb...

(Overwhelmed, WARREN hands the paper back to BROWN.)

BROWN: Horrified by their find, and recognizing Lamb, they notified the police of San Pedro. A small package containing cyanide of potassium was found beside the body.

(BROWN turns to look at WARREN, who has turned away.)

BROWN: *(After a moment)* It was his choice.

WARREN: *(Too quickly)* I know.

BROWN: He could have moved—back to Scotland. Or someplace where nobody knew him.

WARREN: Quiet.

BROWN: I'm trying—

(BROWN *touches* WARREN *almost tenderly.* WARREN *recoils.)*

WARREN: I don't need your comfort!

(WARREN *quietly sheds a tear. It's not feigned. In fact, he may tried to hide it from* BROWN.)

BROWN: Very well. Then let me remind you it was our choice too, pursuing him so avidly. Surely you acknowledge that, Mister Warren.

(No reponse, so BROWN *becomes* SWAFFIELD.)

BROWN/SWAFFIELD: Officer Warren. *(No response)* Officer Warren?

WARREN: *(Recovering)* Oh, yes. I'm sorry, Mister Swaffield.

BROWN/SWAFFIELD: When Lowe visited Brown on the morning of September 26, were there any officers present?

WARREN: *(After a moment)* There were. Officer Hitsman was in the attic with his eye to a hole in the wallpaper.

BROWN/SWAFFIELD: Then your testimony is worthless, for you said earlier that Hitsman was not present on September 26.

WARREN: I did not!

BROWN/SWAFFIELD: What a poor performance, Officer Warren. We all see right through you.

WARREN: Mister Brown, you are overplaying your part so badly, you've made it impossible for me to play mine.

BROWN/SWAFFIELD: Gentlemen of the jury, you don't know these stool pigeons who came here to get our citizens. You do know Lowe, who has been here for ten years. It seems obvious Mister Warren is nothing more nor less than a blackmailer. Whereas Herbert Lowe is a pillar of our community, trusted, relied upon, familiar. Does Mister Lowe look like a degenerate capable of horrible enormity? Let me then direct your gaze to "Officer" Warren. Look at the man who asks you to believe his testimony. See the puffs beneath the eyes, the sallow complexion, the sleek-combed and oiled hair, the pink-manicured finger nails—there is the degenerate. You will recall from testimony that one man was arrested while attempting to go down on Officer Warren. I hesitate to sully your imaginations with this image, but in order to bring a gentleman to his knees, how much "acting" would Officer Warren resort to? Was he not, instead, a willing participant in the crime, an abettor, an instigator? In short, honored jurors, these men, Warren and Brown, are not to be believed by you. Their fingers are dripping with the blood of John Lamb.

BROWN/FISHER: (*Reading*) Jury acquits?! Long Beach florist freed of hideous charge?! Mister McClatchy, look!

WARREN: What?

BROWN/FISHER: (*Reading*) Although five witnesses testified that he was guilty, and four swore that he confessed to the charge in their presence, Herbert N Lowe was acquitted of the charge of vagrancy today in Police Court.

WARREN: No, wait—

BROWN/FISHER: *Los Angeles Times*, December 10, 1914.

(*No reaction from* WARREN.)

BROWN: (*After a moment*) Exonerated!

WARREN: (*Stunned*) Not guilty!

BROWN: We were wrong to do it, Mister Warren.

WARREN: I can't believe it.

BROWN: What now? What's your next scheme?

WARREN: Let me think—

BROWN/SWAFFIELD: I told you I'd get you off, Herbert! Floral tributes everywhere!

WARREN: Let me think—!

BROWN/SWAFFIELD: Herbert? We're celebrating your bravery fighting the charge.

WARREN: Let me think!

BROWN/FISHER: Mister Lowe, I'm Eugene Fisher from *The Sacramento Bee*—

WARREN: What? Who?

BROWN/FISHER: Mister Lowe, *The Sacramento Bee* congratulates you on your acquittal.

WARREN/LOWE: Of course. *The Sacramento Bee*.

BROWN/FISHER: The jury reached its verdict in less than half an hour.

WARREN/LOWE: It is a great relief.

BROWN/FISHER: What do you think convinced them so quickly of your innocence?

WARREN/LOWE: We're all guilty of something, Mister—?

BROWN/FISHER: Fisher. But you may call me Eugene.

WARREN/LOWE: Very well, Eugene. Surely you yourself are guilty of somesuch?

BROWN/FISHER: I beg your pardon? I was asking about—

WARREN/LOWE: Most reporters I know have their secrets, too.

BROWN/FISHER: Our readers are interested in *your* story, Mister Lowe.

WARREN/LOWE: Oh, Eugene, please call me Herbert. By the way, you don't seem like a Eugene to me.

BROWN/FISHER: What?

WARREN/LOWE: Not at all. A Julian, an Oscar, an Algernon, but never Eugene.

BROWN/FISHER: In any case—

WARREN/LOWE: You look very familiar to me. Surely I know you from somewhere—

BROWN/FISHER: That's highly unlikely. I'm based in Sacramento.

WARREN/LOWE: Ah. But I do get up there for nursery business on occasion. Some of our best growers are in the delta. *(He smiles pleasantly but dangerously.)*

BROWN/FISHER: Now, Mister Lowe—

WARREN/LOWE: Herbert!

BROWN/FISHER: You are evading the question, sir!

WARREN/LOWE: I'm the one should be questioning you, Mister Brown.

BROWN/FISHER: Brown—no, I'm Fisher, Eugene Fisher—

WARREN/LOWE: What have you to say for yourself, *Jesus* Brown?

BROWN/FISHER: I'm interviewing you for *The Sacramento Bee*—an exclusive—

WARREN/LOWE: Is that correct? Is *Jesus* your Christian name?

(BROWN can't answer.)

WARREN/LOWE: Mister Brown? Officer Brown? Do you still retain the title, or are you once again merely a thespian? My, I'm full of questions, aren't I? None of them important, in the long run. Except...love. Do actors love, Mister Eugene *Jesus* Fisher Brown? Anyone other than themselves, I mean. Isn't this a question you in fact ask yourself?

BROWN/JESUS: Yes.

WARREN/LOWE: How difficult it must be to fall in love when who you are changes day to day, hour to hour, conversation by conversation! How impossible to be loved by—or to love—an actor!

BROWN/JESUS: It's possible.

WARREN/LOWE: But you wouldn't know—you've never loved an actor, have you, *Jesus*?

BROWN/JESUS: No—I—I didn't have to come here.

WARREN/LOWE: No, you did not.

BROWN/JESUS: I wanted—

(WARREN/LOWE *just stares.*)

BROWN/JESUS: It wasn't—

WARREN/LOWE: It wasn't your idea, *Jesus*? Of course not. That's not who you are. But Mister Warren—Officer Warren—

BROWN/JESUS: It's not what you think!

WARREN/LOWE: Think, my lord? Is he not honest?

BROWN/JESUS: Honest, my lord?

WARREN/LOWE: Honest? Ay, honest.

BROWN/JESUS: My lord, for aught I know.

WARREN/LOWE: By heaven, thou echo'st me,
As if there were some monster in thy thought
Too hideous to be shown!

BROWN/JESUS: He's not a monster!

WARREN/LOWE: What is he then?

BROWN/JESUS: Like mercury, always taking new shapes, you squeeze him and he's gone—

WARREN/LOWE: How can you love quicksilver?

(At the same time:)

BROWN/JESUS: I don't love—!

WARREN/LOWE: It's poison.

BROWN/JESUS: He doesn't just act—he *acts*.

WARREN/LOWE: Takes action?

BROWN/JESUS: He makes things—

WARREN/LOWE: Out of nothing.

BROWN/JESUS: He makes things happen. Monstrous things, sometimes, yes, out of nothing but accent and gesture. He seems in love with surfaces, but I think they betray him—in aping kindness he lays bare his own hidden heart.

WARREN/LOWE: *(After a moment)* Don't ever tell him that.

BROWN/JESUS: He needs to know he's better than he thinks.

WARREN/LOWE: Why, I do believe—

BROWN/JESUS: And he's wrought great change in me. I'm a different person because of him!

WARREN/LOWE: I do believe you're in love with me!

BROWN/JESUS: What, no, of course not—!

WARREN: You are. You as much as said so, Mister Brown.

BROWN: Herbert?

WARREN: Warren. *(Silence. He grins, triumphant.)*

BROWN: Oh, Mister Warren. I didn't realize it was you.

WARREN: *Perhaps* it's me. How would you ever know, I'm so quicksilver?

BROWN: I didn't mean—

WARREN: Never mind all that.

BROWN: You haven't won—what I said to Lowe—you made me—!

WARREN: Grace in defeat, sir. Then onto the next battle.

BROWN: Next battle? Isn't our contest over?

WARREN: Over? What's the fun in that?

BROWN: Mister Warren—

WARREN: I've made appointments for us with the police departments of Venice—

(BROWN *is silent.*)

WARREN: The police department of Venice, Mister Brown—

BROWN: *(Sales pitch)* As Chief of Police, you're undoubtedly well aware—

WARREN: Santa Monica—

BROWN: My partner, Mister Warren, and I have almost single-handedly wiped out vice in the city of Long Beach—

WARREN: Portland—

BROWN: Our method is simple, but effective, and the perversity we've uncovered there would astonish you—

WARREN: And San Francisco—

BROWN: But your own city is certainly the same, for such is the nature of men.

WARREN/MCCLATCHY: We've won, Fisher! We've goddamnn won at last!

BROWN/FISHER: What've we won, sir?

WARREN/MCCLATCHY: *(Handing* BROWN/FISHER *a piece of paper)* Our campaign has triumphed over filth! The Twentieth Century Way is at last a crime in the State of California.

BROWN/FISHER: *(Reading)* The acts technically known as fellatio and cunnilingus are hereby declared to be felonies and any person convicted of the commission of either thereof shall be punished by imprisonment in the state prison for not more than fifteen years. California Penal Code number 288a. Added by the State, 1915.

WARREN: Mister Brown, we've changed the world!

BROWN: California, anyways.

WARREN: Imagine it—*actors* changed the world!

BROWN: Someday we could be President.

WARREN: You could indeed, Mister Brown. You have all the attributes. I've seen your talents grow before my eyes.

BROWN: With your deft instruction. But have we acted properly, Mister Warren? Morally?

WARREN: Our actions have become law. Society is in complete accord.

BROWN: On the surface. But does this feel right to you?

WARREN: *(Taking off his shirt)* My dear Mister Brown, if everyone went around acting on their feelings, we'd have murder and madness. It's oftimes proper to enact the opposite of our feelings for society's sake!

BROWN: But is society always right? Is the majority always right?

WARREN: The majority always *wins.* Now, with The Twentieth–Century Way officially illegal, our services will be in great demand. But our technique needs honing.

BROWN: It's worked reasonably well so far.

WARREN: *(Taking off shoes and socks)* A percentage of our prey escapes—

BROWN: Prey—?

WARREN: And with the change in law, they'll be ever more wary. We'll need to completely embody the role in order to win their trust.

BROWN: What more can we do?

WARREN: Repulsive as it may sound, we must progress further down the path of seduction.

BROWN: Further than The Twentieth–Century Way?

WARREN: I try to stay a century ahead.

(WARREN starts caressing BROWN.)

BROWN: What are you doing, sir?

WARREN: An exercise.

BROWN: Acting.

WARREN: We'll never achieve optimal performance without rehearsal. If you can maintain a professional demeanor, sir, unclouded by emotion, your fear of—

(WARREN intensifies his physical exploration of BROWN, starting to take off BROWN's clothes as well as his own.)

BROWN: Mister Warren—!

WARREN: You're the one who wanted to strip down to the naked truth.

BROWN: That isn't what I meant—!

WARREN: Your words, Mister Brown!

BROWN: As I pass each test, you concoct another more absurd!

WARREN: Do I detect uncertainty, apprehension, dread?

BROWN: Real emotions—yes!

WARREN: Roused by my performance, yet here unmoved I stand. *(Pause)* Who are *you*, Mister Brown? What is it *you* want?

BROWN: Very well, Mister Warren, I will proceed. But we must meld your external technique with my inner method.

WARREN: How, Mister Brown? They are the opposite.

BROWN: Blend them into a new, unified style.

WARREN: Improve improvisation? Impossible!

BROWN: A simple kiss might break down resistance.

WARREN: Oh, no.

BROWN: It's a gesture, but intimate, face to face, profoundly and uniquely human—

WARREN: No kissing, Mister Brown! That's the one thing that will distinguish us from them.

BROWN: Distinguish you from Herbert Lowe?

(BROWN begins to respond physically to WARREN, gradually taking the lead in the seduction. More clothes come off.)

WARREN: Exactly! I created the kissing trait for him to show my range, how far I could go from myself—

BROWN: Herbert Lowe came from within you.

WARREN: Nonsense—he was but a flamboyant—gesture.

BROWN: He was unashamed and unafraid. He would have kissed me, but you stopped him with your slip. He is the best of you.

WARREN: Flattery or insult, Mister Brown?

BROWN: I saw your soul, Herbert—

WARREN: I'm not he!

BROWN: I saw your heart when you shed a tear for John Lamb.

WARREN: He was most...sympathetic.

BROWN: And you regret destroying him.

WARREN: He deserved—

BROWN: And you'd make amends if you could.

WARREN: He's dead—I can't—

BROWN: The line between the actor and role blurs and turns hazardous. Have we become our parts? Gotten emotionally involved?

WARREN: *(Recovering)* Certainly not!

BROWN: Have we been acting too long?

WARREN: We're keeping the performance fresh by introducing new elements.

BROWN: Improvising.

(WARREN starts pushing BROWN's face toward his crotch. They are by now both naked.)

WARREN: Sharpening the edge.

BROWN: We've played so many roles.

WARREN: And so admirably.

BROWN: With such commitment.

WARREN: Admirable commitment, Mister Brown.

BROWN: But it's still just an audition, isn't it?

WARREN: Life is an audition, Mister Brown.

BROWN: And we'll do anything to get the part?

WARREN: You know how casting works.

BROWN: I'm learning.

(Unseen by WARREN, BROWN *takes out the black marking pen.)*

WARREN: A quick study.

BROWN: Indeed I am.

*(*BROWN *quickly marks an X on* WARREN*'s penis.)*

WARREN: You—fucker!

BROWN: *(Shrugs)* Improvisation.

WARREN: This—you—went too far.

BROWN: To the end.

WARREN: You think it's funny? That ink's indelible.

BROWN: Evidence.

WARREN: Sharp. You got the part.

BROWN: Which part?

WARREN: The confidence man.

BROWN: I want more than that, Mister *(Real name of the actor playing* WARREN*)*.

WARREN: That's my—

BROWN: Real name, yeah. And call me *(Real name of the actor playing* BROWN*)*.

WARREN: What the hell are you doing? What do you want?

BROWN: What everyone wants. What Herbert Lowe wants.

WARREN: Love?

BROWN: *(Laughing)* No. But this masquerade—this lie has to end, this—

WARREN: Acting?

BROWN: I want the truth.

WARREN: The truth?

BROWN: Who you are.

(Incredulous, WARREN *gestures: "I'm naked, what more can I show you?")*

WARREN: How—?

BROWN: I want a kiss.

WARREN: A kiss?

BROWN: From *(Real name of actor playing* WARREN*).*

WARREN: If I give you a kiss—in front of all these people who know our real names—

BROWN: We'd no longer be acting.

WARREN: It would be pornography!

BROWN: Unashamed. Naked. Truth.

WARREN: How do you know that's what you want?

BROWN: I'll know it when I see it.

WARREN: You win, Mister *(Real name of actor playing* BROWN*).*

BROWN: No, Mister *(Real name of actor playing* WARREN*),* you do.

(They kiss. It's passionate and unfeigned, raw. Lights fade.)

END OF PLAY

www.ingramcontent.com/pod-product-compliance
Lightning Source LLC
Chambersburg PA
CBHW052209090426

42741CB00010B/2468